A STEP-BY-STEP
TRAINING PARROTS

CAROL J. THIEM with FERN VAN SANT, D.V.M.
and SUZANNE HOPKINS, Behavior Consultant

Photos by co-author Carol J. Thiem: Front cover upper and lower left; title page; 5; 7; 8; 11; 12; 15; 16; 19; 21; 22; 24; 26; 33; 35; 36; 38; 41; 43; 44; 46; 47; 48; 53; 55; 57; 58; 61; 63; 64.

Additional photography: Rebecca Brega, Isabelle Francais, Michael Gilroy, Robert Pearcy, Elaine Radford, R. Williams.

Humorous drawings by Andrew Prendimano.

Title page: A blue-fronted Amazon parrot. Training your pet parrot can be a highly rewarding experience if you exhibit patience and understanding toward your bird.

Distributed in the UNITED STATES by T.F.H. Publications, Inc., One T.F.H. Plaza, Neptune City, NJ 07753; in CANADA to the Pet Trade by H & L Pet Supplies Inc., 27 Kingston Crescent, Kitchener, Ontario N2B 2T6; Rolf C. Hagen Ltd., 3225 Sartelon Street, Montreal 382 Quebec; in CANADA to the Book Trade by Macmillan of Canada (A Division of Canada Publishing Corporation), 164 Commander Boulevard, Agincourt, Ontario M1S 3C7; in ENGLAND by T.F.H. Publications, PO Box 15, Waterlooville PO7 6BQ; in AUSTRALIA AND THE SOUTH PACIFIC by T.F.H. (Australia) Pty. Ltd., Box 149, Brookvale 2100 N.S.W., Australia; in NEW ZEALAND by Ross Haines & Son, Ltd., 82 D Elizabeth Knox Place, Panmure, Auckland, New Zealand; in the PHILIPPINES by Bio-Research, 5 Lippay Street, San Lorenzo Village, Makati, Rizal; in SOUTH AFRICA by Multipet Pty. Ltd., P.O. Box 35347, Northway, 4065, South Africa. Published by T.F.H. Publications, Inc. Manufactured in the United States of America by T.F.H. Publications, Inc.

CONTENTS

INTRODUCTION

Parrots are "people-oriented" birds. They thrive on love and are rarely bashful about asking for more attention. These energetic birds need a lot of stimulation and are usually happiest when they are in the center of a busy household. They will repay your love and care by becoming responsive, beautiful pets and life-long friends. Most parrots, when first purchased, are similar to frightened children. Everything in their world just changed. As a result, they can be fearful and moody. With time, understanding and love, you will be able to transform your withdrawn pet into the colorful, lively friend that a parrot is meant to be. Your relationship with your pet will be much more satisfying when your parrot trusts you and wants to be with you.

There are few hard and fast rules about how to tame or train a parrot. Each bird has its own unique personality which has been shaped by many experiences prior to the day you brought it home. Patience and love are the most important aspects of any training program. This book will offer you procedures and ideas that have worked for other trainers. It will also describe typical responses of parrots to the training procedures so you will have an idea of how your bird might react. However, the key is to observe your bird. It will show you when it is comfortable with you and when it fears your actions or closeness. Be willing to adjust your training program to fit your bird's response.

Try not to have any expectations about how quickly your bird will tame. There are no guidelines for any individual bird. Some cockatoos, for example, have been known to hand-tame and become affectionate in two days. Other individual birds take many months. My lesser sulfur-crested cockatoo has lived with me for ten months and just recently rewarded me by cautiously taking a toy from my hand. Each bird may quickly learn to sit on your hand but reject any of your attempts to pet it for several months. It may backslide. One day your pet will confidently step onto your hand; then the next time you approach the cage, it may withdraw to the back corner and quiver in fear. Be patient. The path will not be straight, but you will train your pet. The results will be worth the effort.

Regardless of its level of training, a parrot can be a fun com-

Three of the author's parrots—a blue and yellow macaw, a blue-fronted Amazon, and a salmon-crested cockatoo. All species of parrot are beautiful and entertaining in their own individual ways.

panion. You can enjoy your bird for the color and life that it brings into your home, whether it cautiously observes the household from a safe distance or boldly struts through your living room as if it owns everything it sees!

BASICS

Whether you have just selected the parrot of your choice and do not know where to start or you have had the bird for a long time and want some new training ideas, you should start with the basics—trust and health. It is unfortunately true that most parrots will be lacking in both areas. Parrots are very hardy creatures, but by the time they have reached the pet store they may have been through some very difficult times. They are going to need tender loving care to restore them to their normal vigor.

There are two general classifications of parrots: wild-caught and domestically raised. Typically, you will be starting with a stronger and healthier bird if you choose to purchase a domestically raised parrot. Wild-caught parrots are more widely available than domestically raised birds and are often less costly, but these birds have generally been traumatized by the experience of being captured and imported. There is also a larger chance of purchasing a sick bird if you select a wild-caught parrot.

Wild-caught parrots are netted in the jungles or plains of their native country and usually placed in crowded cages. There is no assurance that the bird will be placed with other members of its own family or even its own species. The experience of being caught and forced into a cage is very stressful for these wild birds. If they are provided sufficient food, it is often not what they would normally eat. The birds are then transported to a port, sold to an exporter and brought into the country.

A domestically raised parrot, by contrast, may have been sold to you or to the pet store directly by the breeder. There is a better chance that the bird has been well managed. If the bird is labeled a "hand-fed baby," the bird was raised by people instead of its parents. There is a good chance that this bird will be an exceptionally trusting, gentle and affectionate pet.

Opposite: A blue and yellow macaw. Before purchasing a parrot, check it for signs of parasites and illness. The beak, eyes, and feathers should all be clean and in good shape.

A lovely scarlet macaw. Keep in mind that parrots instinctively try to hide signs of illness; because of this fact, a veterinary check-up is vital when it comes to making sure that you are purchasing a healthy bird.

HEALTH CHECK

For your financial protection, we strongly recommend that you purchase your bird with a guarantee that it can be returned in two or three days for a full refund pending the outcome of a visit to a veterinarian. Any responsible pet store will agree to this arrangement; however, you will have to pay for the veterinary bill. Some pet stores will ask you to sign a receipt stating that the bird is sold "as is" before they will allow the bird to leave the premises. Beware. Birds are masters at masking any signs of illness until they are so ill that they can no longer tolerate the stress. You will probably not be able to tell if you have purchased a sick bird unless you are quite experienced with parrots.

Remember that all parrots are wild animals, regardless of how beautifully trained or how many generations have been bred in captivity. Nature has taught them to hide all symptoms of illness to help them survive. In the wild, an obviously sick bird is more likely to be attacked by predators since it appears to be an easy meal. Its own flock may banish the sick bird in order to avoid attracting those predators near other members. Your bird does not understand that hiding symptoms of illness is not an advantage when it lives with people. Unlike your dog or cat, a bird is not domesticated. It can only follow nature's instructions.

To the untrained eye, almost all birds look healthy. The signs of stress or illness are usually quite subtle. A sick bird may continue to eat and move around its cage until its death. This is why it is so important that you take a bird to a veterinarian before you purchase it. If you do notice obvious signs of illness such as coughing, runny nose, rasping or the inability to stay on the perch, the bird is seriously ill. Immediate treatment is necessary.

If you have any other birds in your home, keep your latest arrival completely isolated from them for at least six weeks. Because birds can be contagious without showing obvious symptoms, you run the risk of infecting your other birds if you introduce a new parrot without first insuring that it is healthy. The quarantine period is recommended even after the veterinarian has indicated that your bird is healthy. Your new pet will need this time to adapt to its new home and taming before coping with the stress of establishing its place in the hierarchy of your other birds. If the new arrival shows no signs of distress at the conclusion of your quarantine period, it is likely that the bird will not pose a health threat to your other birds.

A QUIET WELCOME HOME

The first few days after you bring your new parrot home are for getting acquainted and for observation. Help your pet adjust to its new home by placing its cage in a quiet location where it can safely observe the daily happenings in your home without being in the middle of them. Corners are generally best because the bird does not have to observe all directions at once. It knows two directions are safe. This spot need not be the final location of your bird's cage. You can always move it, after the bird is settled, to a location which works better within the layout of your home.

Your bird may be quite upset by the move from the pet store or breeder to your home. Everything in its world has just changed. Your parrot may cower in the farthest corner of its cage or display its agitation by frantically climbing about. If your bird appears to be unsettled by the move, keep your household quiet for the first few days and approach the cage as little as possible. As the bird becomes more comfortable in your home, it will tend to spend more time sitting on its perch, eating, or observing its new home with interest rather than fear. As you observe these changes, you can let your household gradually return to normal.

ENHANCE YOUR PET'S WELL-BEING

At any point after your bird arrives at your home, you can take steps to greatly improve the chances of successfully taming and training your parrot by improving the bird's well-being. One of the easiest steps is to ensure that your parrot always gets at least eight hours of sleep per night. Ten hours maybe preferred. Parrots sleep soundly at night and need that sleep to maintain their health. If the bird's cage is in a busy part of your home, you may want to move it to a quieter location just for the night or cover the cage to isolate the bird from the activity and to darken the interior. The cover will also insure that your bird is warm enough. Your friend will be much more perky after a good night's sleep. Please remember that your bird will awaken at sunrise, regardless of what time the cover is removed from its cage. If you prefer to stay up late and start your day at mid-morning, please put your friend to bed early.

Good nutrition is the next step. If your friend is used to eating only seeds, do not add to its initial stress by changing its diet to unfamiliar food as soon as you bring it home. However, within a month, introduce more healthy foods into the diet and gradually lower the amount of seeds to an occasional treat. Unfortunately, most people think that birds are supposed to eat seeds. In the wild, parrots eat almost none. Seeds provide the bird excessive amounts of fat and lack sufficient vitamins, proteins and minerals. Your bird can survive on an all-seed diet for several years, but it will not thrive as it could on a healthier diet. By contrast, a healthy diet is made up of mostly vegetables and fruits and grains, with supplements of meat and dairy products.

Entertainment also enhances any parrot's well being. Parrots are intelligent and curious birds. They love to have new toys to dismantle and climbing trees to explore. Their need to chew is almost insatiable. Have lots of sticks or toys available for them to chew and keep your furniture and curtains out of reach. Parrots respond well to music and almost any activity. My parrots are at their peak form whenever I have a dinner party. They act as though all these people came to be their audience.

Don't forget showers, sunshine and fresh air! A trip outside (in a cage) to stretch their wings in the fresh breeze can be a joy. Try

Opposite: A lesser sulfur-crested cockatoo. A nutritious and interesting diet will go a long way toward keeping your pet happy and healthy.

gently sprinkling them with the garden hose and watch them arch and stretch to get wet all over. If it is too cold outside, they will enjoy the humidity in the bathroom from your shower.

CLIP YOUR PARROT

There is one important step you should take before you begin to train. Have your parrot's flight feathers clipped. A bird that can fly will fly. The bird would much rather get away from you than be trained to sit on your hand. Additionally, a parrot which has the ability to fly anywhere will challenge your dominance. In the bird's natural world, each bird strives for the highest possible position in the flock. A strong, healthy parrot will challenge you for dominance since you are now its only flock. In order to successfully train this bird, you must be in the dominant position. Clipping your bird's wings is an important part of being certain that the bird knows that you are in control. If the parrot is in control, it will think that you are the one to be trained.

Many people resist wing-clipping because they feel that they are restricting the bird's freedom. Realize that you accepted that your friend could not be free the moment that you purchased it as a pet.

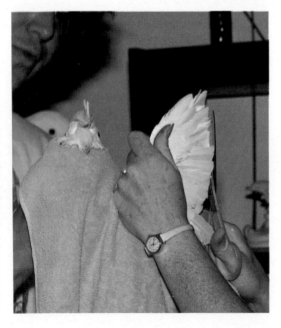

Lesser sulfur-crested cockatoo. If you don't feel comfortable with clipping your pet's wings, have your vet or an experienced bird handler perform this task for you. If you do plan to clip the wings yourself, have an assistant hold the bird for you—don't try to do it alone (especially at first!).

Clipping the wings is a means to ensure the safety of your parrot while it lives in your home. Free flight in a home is dangerous. For example, birds do not understand that windows have glass in them. Seeing the freedom outside, they may try to fly through the window and, instead, they will fly into a glass pane at full speed. Windows are not the only hazard. If the parrot is startled, it may take to the air without a flight plan. Frightened parrots are usually so intent on getting away from the fearful situation that they forget to look where they are going. Crashes are almost inevitable. By contrast, clipped birds will flutter safely to the floor. They still have enough of their flight feathers to allow them to break their fall, but they cannot gain enough speed to injure themselves.

Wing-clipping is a very routine event and you can do it at home, if you choose. It is helpful to have a veterinarian or a trained bird handler clip the bird the first time so that you can observe the proper technique. Wing-clipping does not hurt the bird since there are no nerves in the feathers. It is very similar to cutting hair. However, be prepared for the possibility of holding an angry bird when you clip its wings. Some parrots hate this procedure. Others will be docile. Think of the range of reactions of small children when they have their hair cut and you will understand your bird's feelings.

We recommend that you have both wings clipped. If only one is clipped, the bird cannot control the direction of its flight and is more likely to crash into something. Some trainers prefer a single wing-clip because they believe that the bird knows it cannot fly well and will not try. We are uncomfortable with this thinking because we have seen too many birds take off in a moment of panic without any thought of where they are going. When you have the wings clipped, ask the handler to clip the flight feathers one-half inch below the coverlet feathers. This length will allow sufficient protection for emerging feathers (blood feathers). A broken blood feather will bleed quite severely.

While you are having the wings clipped, you may also want to have the toenails clipped and filed for your comfort. Parrots' toenails get very sharp. They tend to wear into needle-sharp points which aid the bird in climbing in the wild. Such sharp nails are not needed in the home you have provided for your pet. When you succeed in coaxing the bird onto your hand or arm, you do not want to ruin the moment by being startled because you got scratched. I failed to have one of my bird's nails clipped only once. For several days after a parrot training session, my friends were debating whether I had just purchased a kitten or got into a fight with a rose bush and lost!

The very first step in the training process is getting the bird used to your presence. Does your new pet scream in fear when you approach or calmly watch you hoping that you will open that cage door? If your bird remains on its perch or comes to the front of its cage when you come to visit, you are ready to go on and introduce your bird to the larger world outside its cage.

TAMING

It is not uncommon for a newly purchased parrot to try everything possible to get away from you. It may retreat to the back corner and quiver. It may scream and throw itself around the cage in blind panic or fury. Or it may just act very nervous and agitated whenever you enter the room. Don't be discouraged. Your bird just needs time to accept you.

Approach the cage slowly and watch your pet's reactions as you near it. How close can you get? Does the bird panic when you enter the room or will it allow you to be within five feet before it gets nervous? Get as close as the bird allows you. When the bird begins to show signs of nervousness, stop and just quietly talk to your pet. Show it that you don't mean any harm. Spend five or ten minutes visiting from this distance and observe your pet. Is it still hiding in the corner or has it decided that it is safe to climb back onto its perch? Is it listening to you or is it still nervously climbing in circles? After this short visit, leave the bird and go on with your other activities. It is best to train in many short sessions and allow your pet time to rest between them.

Your pet's behavior will tell you whether you can get any closer to the cage the *next* time you approach. If you do succeed in calming the bird with your voice, resist the temptation to continue to approach the cage during that session. You just had a major success! Quit while you are ahead. If you creep forward, you will again make the bird nervous as you push its current limits. It is always best to close any session with a success, because the ending will be what is remembered.

Should your pet not calm down after five or ten minutes, quietly back away and try again from the same distance in a few hours. In time, your pet will understand that you are not trying to harm it and will allow you to come closer.

The difficulty with this early training is that there are times in which you must reach into the cage whether your pet likes it or not.

A tame blue-fronted Amazon coming out of its cage on its owner's hand. Keep in mind that your new pet needs time to get used to your presence.

The bird must be fed and watered. When you must go so close to your fearful pet, keep your movements steady and just do the task you need to do. Do not mix in a bit of training since you seem to have a good opportunity at hand. Your pet has not accepted this intrusion into its cage. Keep your intentions clear. Your pet can understand your intentions through your movements. If you do not take advantage of this situation, you will enhance the trust you are working to develop. Once you have completed your task, leave quietly and let the parrot relax. Wait at least 30 minutes before you attempt to approach the cage in an effort to tame your bird.

Continue with this taming effort and talk to your pet until it calmly accepts your presence when you are standing right next to its cage. In most cases, this process should just take a day or two. A few birds, who have been quite traumatized by previous experiences, may require several weeks before they calm. Don't get frustrated if it seems to take forever and the poor bird screams in fright whenever you enter

Lesser sulfur-crested cockatoo. Allowing your pet to have time outside its cage before formal training begins helps it to feel more at home in its new surroundings. Don't try to begin training immediately.

the room. Many successfully tamed parrots have started this way. Your pet can become a very loving friend. It is just very frightened and needs a lot of patience from you to help it accept its new home. One day, the bird will surprise you by accepting your presence. On that day, you will feel as though someone just gave you a treasured gift.

OPENING THE CAGE

Once your bird allows you to be near, it is time to give your friend the opportunity to explore the world outside its cage. Let your bird take the big step of leaving its home at its own pace. Before you open the door, check that all doors and windows are closed so your pet cannot escape. Pick a quiet time when other pets and family members are not around to frighten your bird. Then open the door of the cage and quietly move away. Some birds are very anxious to get out of the confines of their cage and will emerge immediately. Other birds may take several days to gather their courage and tentatively step outside.

Most birds will naturally climb to the top of their cage when they decide to leave the security of the inside. This is the desired spot for your bird. To encourage your bird to stay in this location, you can provide a bird playground or free-standing perch that can only be reached from the top of the cage.

Your pet can remain outside its cage as long as you desire. The bird will enjoy being outside the confines of its cage and will probably want to remain "free" for as long as possible. Leave the cage door open so your parrot can return to the security of its cage whenever it chooses. You can leave the pet's food and water inside to encourage the bird to return.

It is safest to watch a parrot whenever you allow it free time. Your home is filled with wonderful toys to chew and climb. Those drapery rods are excellent perches and the drapes offer a convenient way to reach that perch. Lamps are also tall and lamp shades are so easy and fun to chew. Your wood furniture is more challenging to carve, but it offers a wonderful way to "whittle" away the hours. You can definitely teach your parrot what areas are off limits, but start the process by watching the bird and preventing any destruction of your belongings.

In most cases, it is very easy to get a parrot back into its cage when it is still unsure of you and its surroundings. Often just approaching the cage will cause the bird to hurry inside. As the bird heads for home, firmly repeat the phrase "Go home" or "Go into your cage." If you repeat this phrase each time, your parrot may eventually associate your words with the action of returning to its cage. Some parrots make this association very quickly and hurry home when commanded. This is very convenient, especially when the bird is not yet hand-trained.

Some birds will decide that it would be more fun to explore your house by wandering all over on the floor. This is not a safe activity. Your pet may decide to nibble on an electric cord or sample the lead weights in your full-length drapes. It will be easier to control and train your pet in the future if you immediately begin to teach the bird that the floor is off limits.

If your pet decides to explore your floor, get a large towel to capture it. You will need to return the bird to its cage immediately. Never use your bare hands or gloves. The bird will hate the thing that captured it. You do not want the bird to hate or fear your hands. It should only associate your hands with comfort. Gloves and hands look the same to the bird and are an identifiable thing that the bird can attack or recoil from in fear. A towel is just an amorphous thing. It can be hated, but a towel lying in a heap on the floor will not cause fear.

When the bird is running across the floor or finds itself in a corner, gently cover it with the towel, insuring that you have covered the head. There is an excellent chance that you will be bitten if you do not cover the head. Let the bird bite the towel. That will help it to relieve its tensions and keep its beak busy. Quickly wrap the towel around its body. Now, supporting its body, gently pick the bird up in the towel and return it to the cage. Carefully loosen the towel and let the bird back out of it. The bird is likely to be very frightened or angry from this treatment, so be as gentle and supportive as possible.

If you simply cannot get close enough to your bird or you are very uncomfortable trying to catch it, don't panic. This will only frighten your parrot and make it harder to get it back inside its cage. Try turning off all of the lights and closing all of the curtains. Parrots become more docile in the dark. In the low light, you should be able to get closer to the bird and gently gather it up in a towel.

INFORMAL TRAINING

Being outside the cage and a part of the happenings in your home is much more fun for these inquisitive and intelligent birds. You will also have more opportunity to interact with a parrot that is not separated from you by the metal of the cage. Much of the taming process happens outside of formal training sessions. Parrots are very "people-oriented" and will be curious about you and your activities. Your bird may come as close to you as the perch allows and then flirt with you. If it is still a bit skittish, it may retreat when you step towards it and then come back to flirt the moment you step away. Most parrots want attention even if they are unsure about being close to you.

You may be able to coax the bird to accept a favorite morsel of food or a new toy from your hand. If the bird backs away, leave the food or toy where the parrot can easily get it. Usually, it will be curious about what you brought and sample it as soon as you are safely away. The parrot knows that you offered it this special thing. The bird will probably watch you closely and know exactly where you placed this treasure. Gradually, you will observe that your friend does not back off quite as far or quite as fast when you offer something. You are proving that you can be trusted.

Daily human activities can be quite entertaining to parrots. They thrive on stimulation. My parrots talk and sing to the sounds of the radio, shower, vacuum cleaner, power saws and any other noise in this crazy household. It really does not matter to them what the source of the sound is—it is just a great excuse to sing along. Parrots can be fascinated by such basics as watching you wash the dishes or play with your children. Dinner guests will often be entertained by ev-

Blue and yellow macaw. Don't allow your newly acquired pet outdoors—this is the best way to lose your parrot. Supervised fresh air and sunshine sessions are a long way off.

ery trick in the book because your little attention-getter has a bigger audience.

Parrots can be great fun at this stage of training even though you may not be able to touch them. As they continue to get more comfortable in your home, their antics become more amusing to watch. You can provide all kinds of toys for them to play with and happily chew to shreds.

Spend time with your bird. It will become a happy, well-adjusted friend if it is given enough love and attention. The formal training only becomes easier as your pet knows you better.

The cornerstone of parrot training is teaching your bird to trust you enough to mount your hand. The physical action itself is very simple for any bird and requires no instruction. Stepping up onto something just a few inches above its feet is no challenge for these acrobatic birds. However, stepping up onto a human hand is much more complicated than just stepping onto another tree branch. The

HAND-TAMING

bird has to trust you enough to allow you to have control over it. Such trust goes against the bird's natural instincts. If your pet was treated harshly before you purchased it, those instincts were unfortunately reinforced by experience. Your training challenge is to teach the bird that you can be trusted.

The best time to begin to hand-tame is just after the parrot is over the initial stress of moving into your house and is willing to leave the security of its cage when you open the door. You want to start training while your pet is still learning about its new environment. At this stage, the bird is still adapting and is not quite secure enough to seek dominance or assume an aggressive stance. It is easier to train a timid bird than a confident, aggressive bird. However, if you have had your bird long enough to be completely at home and you have not started any training program, you can still expect a successful outcome. You may have missed the optimal starting point, but there is no reason why your bird cannot be trained. It may just require a little more patience and perseverance on your part.

It is not necessary for your new pet to like you in order to learn to stand on your hand. It does not even have to like standing on your hand. Your bird just has to do as you have trained it. However, once your pet has learned to trust you enough to get on your hand, you have made it possible for genuine friendship to develop. By contrast, if you decide to have the bird learn to like you before you hand-tame it, you could have a long wait. The bird cannot like you until it gets beyond its natural distrust of people. You have to actively prove to the bird that you mean no harm. Simply feeding the bird regularly and talking to it may not be enough proof. A confident bird may tame under either training method, although it will take much less time if you actively train it. However, a bird which has been traumatized and is especially afraid of people could take years to tame if you wait until

Blue and yellow macaw. The first step in hand-taming is getting your parrot to step onto a stick from the floor.

it is brave enough to climb onto your hand spontaneously.

The easiest and most reliable way to accomplish the goal of having the bird step up onto your hand from any location is to break the behavior into a series of small steps. The first step will be one that the bird is most likely to perform. Then by building on the successful accomplishment of each step, you will guide your pet to performing the behavior you actually want.

Here is the path which we recommend that you follow as you teach your bird to step up on to your hand from any location. Have the bird:

1. Mount a stick from the floor.
2. Stay on the stick.
3. Step from one stick to another.
4. Step from the stick to your hand.
5. Step from a free-standing perch to the stick.
6. Step from the perch to your hand.
7. Step from the top of its cage to the stick.
8. Step from the top of its cage to your hand.
9. Step from the inside of the cage to a stick.
10. Step from the inside of the cage to your hand.

As you work with your pet at each step, praise the bird for everything it does right while the bird is doing the correct behavior. Remember that the bird does not understand exactly what you want it to do and

Red-lored Amazon. Your pet may cower in a corner of the training area as you try to get him to step onto the stick. Soon, however, he will realize that the floor is the last place he wants to be, and he'll mount the stick.

it cannot understand your words of explanation. However, it certainly can understand that it pleased you when it did a certain action, no matter how simple. If you praise or reinforce action that is in the right direction of the behavior you really want, you increase the chances that the action will happen again. As your bird seeks to continue to please you and earn that reinforcement, it will tend to do that action more strongly and more often.

As we discuss each of the steps in detail, we will offer you techniques for working with your bird and its likely reactions to the training. However, you know your individual bird and can observe its reactions to your attempts to train it. Feel free to adjust the methods so that they work for you and your bird. The only goal is for you and your bird to achieve a comfortable relationship that makes both of you happy.

STEP ONE—MOUNT A STICK FROM THE FLOOR

The floor has been selected as the starting point for hand-taming because your bird will not be comfortable there and will want to climb onto anything that is higher. In the wild, birds are very vulnerable on the ground. They feel much more secure when they are perched high in the air. If you hold the only available object that the bird can climb on, your pet will have to get used to the idea that it must accept the fear of being near your hand in order to avoid the discomfort of being on the floor. Usually birds will do anything to get off the floor. Remember, however, that your bird probably fears you almost as much as being on the floor, so be as calm and reassuring as possible.

HAND-TAMING

It is best if you bring the bird to a location in your home where it cannot escape from you. The bathroom is often used. You can also pick a corner of a room and build a small enclosure with boxes or furniture. You can use yourself as the fourth wall or you can go inside the enclosure with your pet. Your training area should be easily cleaned since parrots void frequently, especially when they are nervous. Tile, linoleum and sealed hardwood floors clean up easily. Check your area to be sure that there are no electrical outlets or cords that the bird can reach. Remove any sharp objects that your parrot might hit if it were to move or attempt to fly suddenly.

Have two sticks or dowels handy in the training area. They should be about one-and-a-half to two feet long and the same diameter as your pet's most comfortable perch. Your bird's toes should reach about three-quarters of the way around the stick when the parrot is standing on it. The second stick will be needed in future lessons.

Now, bring the bird to your training area and place it on the floor. Often, this is not an easy task. The bird will know that you plan to do something with it and it will probably decide that it has no intention of leaving its cage. If the cage is small enough, you can bring the entire cage to the training area and then remove the bottom so that the bird must come out. You can also catch the bird in your trusty towel and deliver it to the right location. Carrying the bird in a towel will not hurt it. Regardless of how you deliver the parrot to your training area, it will probably be difficult. For this reason, it is often kindest to quickly capture the bird in a towel, carry it to the room, and release it. The longer you take to remove the bird from its cage, the more you will traumatize your pet. Once you succeed in bringing the bird to the training area, set it on the floor and give it a few minutes to rest before you begin any training.

Your parrot is not going to like being on the floor in this new place. It is very likely that it will anxiously explore the space looking for any possible escape route. It may try to climb onto anything in the space that it has a remote chance of being able to climb. When the bird discovers that it is trapped in this space with you, it may just try to hide in the corner or hide under part of you!

When you are ready to train the bird to mount, approach the bird's abdomen with one of the sticks. Approach the bird at an even height from the floor rather than coming down at the bird. If you approach the bird's head first, your pet will react as if you were trying to attack it. A low approach is much less threatening. You may have to touch your stick to the bird's abdomen before it will willingly step up or mount the offered stick.

Your bird can respond to your offered stick in several ways. It may back up if it touches the wall, run away, step over the stick and flee, or step onto it. The least likely possibility is that the parrot will attempt to bite the stick. Most birds will prefer to get away rather than to attack something larger than them. In all probability, you will spend three to 15 minutes chasing the bird all over the floor of the training space with the stick. This step is difficult for most parrot owners. The bird will put on a very convincing act of being frantic and terrified. You are not hurting the bird. However, you are purposely making the experience of being on the floor very uncomfortable for your pet. Your bird must understand that it gets hassled when it is on the floor. It will soon discover that all of the hassling stops when it mounts the stick. In most cases, you are only 15 minutes from having the bird on the stick when you start this process. This step is the hardest part of the entire training process. It may be an unpleasant time for both you and the bird, but know that you are not damaging your pet or your relationship with it. In just a short time, the bird will do as you have asked.

Red-lored Amazon. Some parrots are easier to tame than others and may be willing to step onto your hand from the floor. Don't rush your pet, however. Let him learn at his own pace.

When your bird becomes brave enough to quickly run over the stick to escape on the other side or just touches the perch with its foot, stop all activity. Let the world be completely calm and quiet for about ten to 15 seconds. Each time your pet is willing to step up onto the stick, no matter how briefly it stays there, stop all movement and noise. Your parrot will quickly understand that standing quietly on the perch is better than being chased on the floor. Do not prevent the bird from jumping off the stick at this stage. Any attempts to constrain the bird would be perceived as threatening. You want the parrot to see your stick as a safe place, not a dangerous place to be avoided. Do not move your hand suddenly when the bird steps up onto the stick. Be very steady.

After the bird has been on the stick for ten seconds, put the bird back on the floor. Repeat the process again even if you have to spend another three minutes chasing the bird around the floor. After a few chases, you will notice that the period of time your bird will choose to spend on the floor will lessen. You have made it more comfortable for your pet to be on the perch. Continue to work with the bird for a total of about 20 minutes and then close the lesson.

If possible, it is best to end a lesson on a positive note. Your pet will tend to remember the last action that it performed. It is far more important to end on a positive than it is to train for a certain length of time. If your pet understands that it should step up on the stick on demand within the first five minutes, congratulate it (and yourself) and end the lesson. You can have another lesson in an hour or so or on another day. It may not always be possible to have a happy ending to each lesson. Your bird may not accept the stick and may spend the entire time trying to get away from you. Don't be discouraged. Work with the bird for 20 minutes, or less if both of you are tired, and end the lesson.

When you decide that the lesson is over, bring the bird back to its cage or play area. Do not allow the bird to escape and find its way back to its cage. If you allow the bird to escape, you have lost control over the bird. It will simply spend all of its lesson time looking for the earliest possible time to escape. In later lessons, you will want to work with your bird within sight of its cage. You don't want your pet to decide when it is time to go home. Begin immediately to ensure that the bird knows that you are in control of the lessons.

STEP TWO—STAY ON THE STICK

After your pet consistently mounts the stick without hesitation, you can allow it to stay on the stick for longer periods. In order

Blue and yellow macaw. Move the stick very slowly and steadily after your bird has perched on it. Be prepared for the parrot to fly off and head for his cage.

to avoid the floor, a parrot is usually willing to stay there when the stick is steady. However, your bird may become concerned when its "perch" begins to move around the room. Tree branches don't move this way!

Introduce the idea of riding on perch by moving the stick very slowly after your bird has become settled on it. Keep the stick an even distance from the floor so that the bird will not have a great distance to jump if it decides that it does not like this kind of ride. Keep talking to your bird. Be careful not to start or stop quickly as you may accidentally jar the parrot off the stick.

Once your bird appears to be willing to hold onto the stick, you can raise the stick higher from the floor. Eventually, you should be able to walk around the training area with the bird perched on the stick and quietly sitting there.

One common problem is that the bird will fly off the stick as soon as you move to a spot which permits a possible escape back to its cage or play area. It will be safe if you only work with the bird within the confines of your selected training area at this time. If the bird does escape, do not chase it. Allow the bird to run until it stops. If it reaches its cage, catch it in the towel and bring it back to the training area. If the parrot stops anywhere before it reaches its cage, you can offer it the stick to mount. Your pet knows that it should climb on the stick in the confines of the training area, but it does not necessarily know that it should do the same action in some other place in your house. If the bird is very frightened or anxious to return home, it may avoid climbing on the stick. You may have to catch the bird in your towel. Regardless of where you regain control over the bird, bring it back to the training area and review the lessons learned. A repeat of these lessons should only take a minute or so, but it does reinforce both the lessons and the rule that *you* determine when a lesson is complete rather than your pet.

STEP THREE—STEP FROM ONE STICK TO ANOTHER

The third step reinforces the mounting process and teaches the bird to perform for you without the hassle and discomfort of being on the floor. Your pet knows how to step up onto the stick. Now you will train the bird to step up because you have asked it to mount and not because of any discomfort. The bird's positive reinforcement is your reassuring voice saying "Good bird" each time your pet performs correctly.

Begin this step by bringing your pet to your training area. Reinforce the earlier lessons by placing the bird on the floor and then having it step up onto your offered stick. If there is any hesitancy, your bird is not ready for this step. Continue working at the previous steps until the bird confidently steps up onto the stick each time you offer

Peach-fronted conure. When teaching your pet to step from one stick to another, always keep the second stick level with the bird's abdomen.

it. Once your pet is comfortable perching and riding on the stick you are holding, pick up a second stick in your hand and approach the bird's abdomen. The approach should be exactly the same as your approach when the bird was on the floor. The action you want is for the bird to calmly step up onto the new stick and quietly perch there.

When your bird accepts this new action, you can repeat it by lowering the stick which the bird is perching on and then offering the original stick at the height of the parrot's abdomen again. If you continue in this manner, you can have the bird walk back and forth between the two sticks. It will believe that it is climbing constantly, but it will actually be going nowhere.

Introduce the command "Step up" now. Each time you offer the next stick, say "Step up." By teaching your pet this command, you will eventually be able to control your pet's actions by voice command. Your bird will respond to your commands by performing the behavior you expect.

This walking exercise is an excellent reinforcement of stepping onto the new perch and a learning tool for the voice command. Continue this exercise for ten to 20 repetitions. Remember, leave each lesson on a positive note. After a few minutes of this exercise, the bird will begin to tire. Stop before the bird simply refuses to continue.

Sometimes, this step does not occur as smoothly as described above. Your bird may regard the new perch with fear and flee from its current one every time the new stick approaches. Try slowing your approach and be sure that the new stick is approaching the bird level with its abdomen. If this does not help, repeat step one for a while. Then sit down on the floor and combine steps one and three. When the bird is on the floor, have it mount the first stick. Congratulate it for doing this action. Then, without raising the original stick, offer the bird the second stick at the height of its abdomen. The bird should be willing to step up on the new stick since you have made the new action almost identical to the one it just accomplished. The only difference is that the bird was standing on a stick rather than the floor. The bonus to your parrot is that it gets to climb a bit higher. Usually, this arrangement is accepted. Once the bird is willing to step onto the second stick, you can offer the original stick and teach the bird to do the stick walking as described above.

If your bird is extremely nervous, spend extra time with it when the bird is in its cage or in its play area. Let it get used to your presence when it knows that you have no lesson plans in mind. The more pleasant interactions you can have with your bird, the less threatened it will feel when you are training it.

Peach-fronted conure. Getting the parrot to step from the stick to your hand is often the most difficult part of the hand-taming process. Take your time.

STEP FOUR—STEP FROM THE STICK TO YOUR HAND

This step is the first time you will ask your pet to step onto your hand. You have prepared your parrot well. It knows all of the motions and what to expect. The only challenge will be that your hand will be substituted for the second stick. This may be a big change for your pet. Even though it knows exactly what to do, it must accept the idea of actually standing on a human hand. However, before you begin this lesson, determine how *you* feel about having this parrot on your hand. Are you afraid of your parrot's beak? If you are, your bird will know it and it is very unlikely that you will succeed in training your bird to mount your hand.

Your actions will convey your feelings to your parrot. Picture the clean movements of a person who simply expects that the parrot will step up onto his hand from the stick. The hand will be steady. The movement will be confident and smooth. The parrot will be offered a firm, reliable perch to stand on and the bird will know this. Now compare those movements with the actions of a person who is thinking, "Please, step up onto my hand and please, please do not bite me." The movement of the hand is likely to be hesitant and jerky. The hand may tentatively approach the bird and then back away. Even the most tame parrot would not want to step onto a perch that unreliable. Certainly, an untamed bird will not.

Peach-fronted conure. After your parrot has successfully mastered stepping from the stick to your hand, you may wish to have him step from one hand to the other.

In order to be completely confident, you are going to have to accept that you will be bitten at some point. It is simply a part of the taming process. No, it is not pleasant and, yes, it can hurt. But you cannot allow yourself to be afraid of it if you want to successfully hand-train your parrot. The way to accept the idea of being bitten is to know what to do when it happens. You do not have to stoically "take it." When the parrot catches your finger in its beak, quickly pull your hand up and away from the bird and say "No!" sharply. The sudden "No!" will usually startle the bird enough for it to let go. By pulling up and away, you are rolling your finger out of the bird's beak. If the bird really wanted to hang on through this action, it would soon find its feet off the ground. No bird wants to bite you that badly. The parrot really wants you to stop doing whatever it was that frightened it. Once you have backed off, the bird will back off.

Now at this point, you are probably angry because your finger has been bitten and it hurts. Control that anger. Do *not* hit the bird. The bad behavior has stopped. You stopped it by exclaiming "No!" and pulling away quickly. If you now hit the bird, you are attacking it out of revenge and the bird learns nothing except that you can and will attack. Leave the bird if you must or just sit quietly until you feel in control again. The bird is not going to continue the attack once you back away. It probably needs more time than you do to calm itself. It may have felt frightened for its life!

Once you both have settled down, you should continue the lesson. It is best if you never end a lesson after the bird has bitten you.

30

If you choose to end the lesson, you have given the parrot control over the length of the lesson. Additionally, you have not closed on a positive note. The bird will remember that it had to bite to defend itself. (So will you!) Go right back to the beginning of the hand-training process and work your way back to the step you were working on when the incident happened. By going back to the basics, you will reassure both the parrot and yourself that the earlier lessons are still understood and no damage has been done to the developing relationship. Depending on how long you both have been working in this session, you can either stop now or go on.

Are you ready to work with your bird or are you still nervous? If you are nervous, find a pet store or a trainer who owns a very tame parrot and allows other people to handle it. Have this parrot mount your hand so that you can get used to the idea of having a bird perching on your hand. Give yourself some time to observe the normal movements and activities of a tame parrot so that you will not feel threatened by the actions of your own bird. Notice that this bird's movements are very similar to your parrot's movements. As you learn more about your pet and other parrots, you will become more comfortable handling and interacting with your bird.

Offer your hand to the bird in the same way that you offer the stick. Be very steady and approach the bird's abdomen. As always, the bird will want to step *up* to a perch rather than down. If your bird is confident, it may step up onto this new "perch" and accept your hand readily. If your training goes this well, continue to work with the bird by offering it the stick again and then your hand. You can then go on to have the bird "walk" between your two hands instead of using the sticks.

A more common reaction of the bird will be fear. As you approach the bird with your hand it may lean as far back as possible to get away from this new menace. As your hand continues to approach, the bird may fly off the stick or try to bite you. Flying away is the usual reaction. When the bird flies away, offer it the stick to climb back up and start over again. Don't forget to talk to your bird and continue to reassure it. Should the bird try to bite you, say "No!" very sharply. Speed up your approach so the bird does not have as much time to get into an attack position. Make it very clear that you expect it to step up onto this perch. When the bird does mount your hand, praise it.

If you find that you and your pet are "stuck" at this stage, there are some tricks that you can try which may help keep the training progressing. You can gradually introduce your hand to the bird by shortening the length of the stick available to the bird. Start by offering the stick to the parrot so that it mounts it. Have the bird walk between the two sticks. Each time you offer the next stick, move your grip up a fraction of an inch so that the length available to your bird is shortened. Eventually, your bird will be standing right next to your hand and may tentatively rest one foot on your finger. Another trick is to try lowering the parrot's end of the stick so that the stick is angled down away from you. Parrots prefer to climb and maintain their height. They are uncomfortable when they are lower than their surroundings, including you! Since your hand is the highest point immediately available, the parrot may climb up onto it.

If you have tried all of our suggestions and your bird just recoils in fear for lesson after lesson, there are other steps you can take. First, let yourself unwind and relax. At some point your bird may have been badly frightened. You will eventually succeed at getting this bird to trust you, but, in this case, you may have to be very patient. Your bird can detect your nerves and any impatience that you feel. Those emotions will only serve to frighten your pet further.

Next, review the environment you have provided for your pet. Is the bird being frightened by a child poking at it or by your big, friendly dog or cat? Can neighboring cats panic your friend by staring at it through a window? Do hawks or other large predatory birds fly near your house where they can be seen by your parrot? My birds dive behind the couch and hide for hours whenever a hawk flies near the house. Is your pet exhausted by being unable to get out of the hot noon sun? If something is amiss, correct it and give your bird a few days to accept that the disturbing situation has been changed. Then restart your lessons.

If nothing appears to be amiss or correcting the problem does not result in any improvement in the bird's response to your lessons, it is time to give the bird a different kind of lesson. Put on some old comfortable clothes and grab a good book. Bring your parrot into the bathroom and set it down in the dry bathtub or shower stall. Then climb in yourself and stretch out. Alternate ten-minutes sessions of talking to your bird with ten minutes of ignoring it and reading your book. The only goal of this exercise is to give the bird sufficient opportunity to get to know you and learn to trust you. It does not matter if the bird stands as far from you as possible and just quivers. Make no moves towards it. Just talk to your little friend for a while and then go back to your book. Spend about an hour with your bird and then return it to its cage or perch. Repeat this exercise every day or so until your bird no longer cowers near you.

Salmon-crested cockatoo. If you are training a larger parrot, such as a cockatoo or macaw, the bird may have to use your forearm rather than your hand.

Eventually, the parrot will begin to get curious about you. It may gingerly reach out to touch your foot or pant leg. Do not pull back suddenly. Just talk softly to your bird to encourage its bravery or ignore it. When the bird demonstrates consistent interest, move your foot slowly. Go slowly with your skittish friend. The bird may jump in fear when you move your foot. That is okay. Your parrot is smart enough to see that you did not attack it. Soon, its curiosity will overcome its fear and it will be back touching your leg. When your little friend takes this step, you know that it is interested in you and trainable. You can now begin to approach the bird with your hand. Proceed with the training described above.

STEP FIVE—FROM FREE-STANDING PERCH TO STICK

When you started training your parrot, the bird was willing to step onto the stick you held because perching on the stick was less threatening than being on the floor. Now you will train your pet to mount the stick when the bird is comfortably perched on a safe free-standing perch. This is a good intermediate step toward the ultimate goal of having your parrot mount your hand on demand from any location. When your pet is on the perch, it does not feel the vulnerability that it felt when you placed it on the floor. However, because you have placed the perch in the training area, your pet only has the options of mounting your stick or fleeing back to the floor when the stick approaches it.

To your bird, this situation is very different than mounting a stick from the floor. When the bird was on the floor, it was very motivated to end the discomfort of feeling vulnerable. The only other option it had was to climb up onto a stick held by a human hand, so it took that option. Being near that hand or on that hand was not a comfortable situation since the bird had no way of knowing your intentions, but at least it was better than having to watch out for every other kind of enemy that could attack from the ground. Now that the parrot is on a perch, it is comfortable. It would be quite happy to stay there. You are making your pet uncomfortable by offering it two unwelcome choices. The bird can either climb onto that stick or flee to the floor. The bird would prefer that you just left it alone on the perch. By working through this lesson, you are helping your pet understand that climbing up onto the stick that you hold is not an uncomfortable option. The bird will learn that it does not have to fear you.

To begin this lesson, you will need a free-standing perch. You can purchase a perch at a pet store that sells parrots. Place the perch in your training area with your training sticks. Bring in your parrot and place it on the floor. Offer the bird a stick and quickly work through the previous lessons to reinforce the training learned so far. Then bring your bird to the perch so that your parrot will have to step up onto it. As you allow the bird to step from your stick to the perch say "Okay" to release the bird. You can use any command you prefer to release the bird, but be sure your choice of command does not sound at all like "Step up." You do not want any confusion between commands.

Usually, parrots are quite anxious to step onto anything which is not attached to a person. Give your friend a few minutes to explore its new temporary home.

Offer the bird a stick just as you have done before and command your pet to "Step up." Your pet may try to run away from the stick by sidestepping back and forth along the perch. Continue to approach the parrot until it is willing to step up onto the stick or it finally flies to the floor. If the bird steps up, congratulate it and show it that you are pleased. Let the bird rest for a moment on the stick. Do a few "walks" between the two sticks and then let the parrot return to the perch. Repeat the exercise.

If the parrot flies to the floor, immediately offer it the stick to mount. Do not allow the bird to relax on the floor. It should only relax when it has mounted your stick. Have it walk between the two sticks and then return the bird to the free-standing perch. Talk to your bird constantly. It needs a lot of reassurance to accept that it must

Blue and yellow macaw. It is most likely that your parrot is quite comfortable on the free-standing perch and may resent your demand that he step onto another stick.

willingly give up its perch to mount your stick. Continue to repeat the exercise until your pet willingly mounts the stick from the perch each time you offer it.

STEP SIX—STEP FROM THE PERCH TO YOUR HAND

After your pet completely understands that it must mount the stick from the perch, offer it your hand. Some birds will immediately accept this step and perform it perfectly on the first try and then go on to repeat the performance each time you offer your hand. Such a bird has probably understood most of the concept that it should always step up onto your hand. Other birds will resist stepping onto your hand. If your bird flees, have it mount the stick and return it to the perch. Repeat the lessons of step five and then offer your hand once again. If this fails after several attempts, return to step four, "mounting your hand from the stick," and reinforce that training. In time, your pet will understand what you are asking of it.

When your bird will reliably step from a free-standing perch to your hand, you are more than half way through the taming process. Congratulations to you both!

Blue and yellow macaw. As you get to know your pet, you will be able to tell when a bite is coming. A brightly colored water pistol or spray bottle is an effective tool for preventing a bite from occurring.

It is now time to begin to work with your pet outside of the training area. Move the free-standing perch to another place in your home. You are ready to give up the training area, but you are not quite ready to work with your bird near its cage. Pick any location that is not within sight of the bird's cage but is reasonably open. Be sure that all windows and doors are closed. Since you may have to retrieve your pet several times, pick a location where furniture can easily be moved and you can tolerate any mess.

Repeat both steps five and six. Work with your pet in this location with both the stick and your hand. Remember to use the voice commands of "Step up" to mount and "Okay" to release your parrot. Reinforce all the good actions by saying "Good bird" whenever the action is performed correctly. In most cases, your pet will perform correctly in this new location. If your bird steps up correctly several times, try walking around your home with the bird perched on your hand. If the bird flies off, return it to the free-standing perch and start over. Have the bird step up onto your hand a few more times and then go for another walk. Walk backwards near the danger spots, such as near its cage, so your pet cannot see the temptation.

Sometimes the freedom and space in the perch's new location will tempt your pet to avoid the training by diving to the floor to escape your hand or the stick. Your pet may know that its cage is not far away. If your pet responds to the new location this way, return the bird to the perch in the towel each time it flies off. Your parrot knows that it should not fly off. By leaving, it has committed itself to being returned in a towel and the bird will not like this treatment. It will quickly realize that stepping up onto your hand is preferable to being toweled.

STEP SEVEN—STEP FROM TOP OF CAGE TO STICK

The next step is to have your bird mount your stick from the top of its cage. Some parrots become so attached to their cages that they only tolerate lessons to get back home. If you now start to bring the bird somewhere interesting when you take it away from its home, the bird will associate your offered hand or stick with excitement and fun.

There are many good places for a parrot to safely enjoy. Perhaps you can place a play area in another room which the parrot can only get to by being carried. This perch can be placed anywhere that you will be working or playing. A separate play area has the advantage of offering new views for your pet. The shower curtain rod in your bathroom is another excellent perch. Parrots often love perching there while someone takes a shower. The steam and high humidity are good for them and the room is usually warm and pleasant. They may regale you with all of their "songs" and "talk" to accompany the noise of the shower or your own songs. My Amazon often "asks" to sit in the bathroom by himself in the evening. I presume he enjoys the peace and quiet and the warmth of the room. We have had a great deal of fun

Peach-fronted conure. Be sure to praise your parrot after he has stepped onto the stick from the top of the cage.

Blue-fronted Amazon. Once your parrot is hand-tamed, he may enjoy perching on the shower curtain in your bathroom. However, be sure all dangerous appliances and chemicals are out of the way before you let the bird into this or any room.

when visitors use the room only to discover that they are being observed by a quiet green parrot perched contentedly on the shower curtain rod. Parrots also like going to an outside cage and enjoy the sunshine and fresh breeze. You can either build an outside aviary or take the cage outside. Be sure that the lock on the cage is secure as it can be difficult, if not impossible, to recover an escaped parrot.

The more you include your pet in your activities, the less it will need the security of its cage and the more willing it will be to accept the offer of your hand or stick. Eventually, your friend will regard its cage as simply a place to sleep.

As a word of caution, there is one room which is potentially very dangerous for your bird's perch or cage—the kitchen. Many people do enjoy their birds in this room, but please be cautious if you choose the kitchen. Kitchens are full of electrical appliances which could be accidentally turned on by a curious parrot. The bird might decide to chew through the cord and could be seriously shocked. Your stove has very hot surfaces that a bird could land on without recognizing the danger. There are also many cooking fumes in a kitchen that may be harmful. Among the most deadly are the toxic fumes from a non-stick pan which is accidentally left on a hot burner and begins to smoke. However, kitchens often have the advantage of being the center of the household activities that your bird will enjoy once it is used to your home. If you choose to have your bird in this room, keep it caged to prevent your pet from landing in something dangerous. An open perch, whether the bird is free or tethered, only invites disaster.

When you are ready to begin the lesson, let your pet out of its cage and have it climb to the top. Most birds, at this stage of training, will climb out immediately once the door is opened. This time, close the door after the bird is out and remove any nearby cages or perches that offer escape routes. Offer the stick to your parrot to mount. If all goes well, the bird will step up onto the stick. However, a more typical reaction is that the parrot will frantically climb around the top and sides of the cage to avoid that stick. If you manage to trap the bird, it may fly to the floor to escape your approach. When your pet is on the floor, it should be comfortable in stepping up onto the stick as it has done many times in its previous training. Once it is back up on your stick, spend a few minutes talking to the bird and calming it. Then bring the bird back to the top of its cage and repeat the exercise.

If your bird insists on climbing around to avoid the stick, you may want to make the cage a little more difficult to climb on. Move the bird to another location and tape paper all over the sides of the cage. The paper will make it very difficult or impossible for the parrot to hold onto the wire sides. You can also use old sheets or other fabrics to cover all but the top of the cage. Once you have limited your parrot's range of travel, bring the bird back to the cage. After you have given it a moment to get used to the changes to its home, offer it the stick to mount. Remember, each time the bird does what you have asked, praise it. When the bird indicates a willingness to leave its cage for the stick you have offered it, repeat the exercise several times to insure that your pet understands. Reward the achievement occasionally by taking the bird to its play area for some relaxation. You can leave the bird there for ten minutes to a half-hour and then continue the lesson.

Once your pet is willing to leave the top of its cage, begin to remove the paper or the fabric a little at a time. Each time a piece is

Peach-fronted conure. Have your pet step right from the top of the cage to your hand if the bird seems to feel comfortable. If not, take the bird out of the training area on the stick and then have him step from the stick to your hand first.

removed, repeat the lesson so that the bird understands that it is still expected to come to you even though it has more opportunity for escape.

Now that you are working with your pet in its own territory, it is very necessary that you end the lesson on a positive note and on your terms. Since the bird is home, it may just want you to leave. When you have determined that the lesson is over, bring the bird to another location for a few minutes. While your pet is away, restore its cage and "home" area to its normal condition. Then bring your parrot back home, preferably riding your stick or your hand. By ending the lesson in this manner, you are making it clear that you are still in control even though you are working with your pet in its territory.

STEP EIGHT—STEP FROM TOP OF CAGE TO HAND

You may be able to achieve this step very quickly after your pet understands that it must come to you from the top of its cage. Your hand should not be threatening any longer. However, some parrots are nervous about stepping on a hand even after they have shown a willingness to step up on to the stick from the top of the cage. In this case, have the bird mount the stick from the cage and then walk away from the area. Work with your pet by having it walk between the stick and your hand. You need not be in the old training area, but just away from the bird's cage. Once your pet is comfortable working this way, return it to the top of the cage and repeat the exercise.

STEP NINE—STEP FROM INSIDE OF CAGE TO STICK

Now you are at the home stretch. A bird that is willing to come out of its cage on a stick held by its owner is almost fully tamed. At this stage, your bird may have the idea that it is just supposed to step on your stick or your hand whenever you offer it regardless of where the bird happens to be. If you can reach into your parrot's cage and have the bird accept a ride outside without trying to grab the side of the cage as it goes by, congratulate both of you! Your pet is hand-tamed. It is possible for your pet to suddenly understand exactly what you wanted all along and bypass several steps of the taming process. It is also possible, and more likely, that your pet will need to work through each step. Don't feel bad; my cockatoo has needed every single step and most of the tricks I have offered to you. The pace truly depends on the individual bird.

If your bird does not have the understanding that it is supposed to step up onto your hand, it will either run frantically around the inside of the cage, try desperately to get out, hide in the farthest

Blue-fronted Amazon. A parrot that is willing to come out of the cage on a stick or hand on demand is almost completely hand-tamed.

corner, or try to bite the menacing hand. The papering trick can work well for the bird that wants to run around the inside of the cage. Remove the bird to its play area. Then paper the inside of the cage—top, bottom and all four sides except for the opening. Place the bird back inside the cage on its perch.

Offer your pet the stick to mount. Your parrot will either sidestep along the perch in its cage or decide it really ought to mount the perch you offer. If the bird tries to get away from your stick, it will find that it cannot climb the sides of its cage to escape because of the paper you have placed there. Once the bird mounts your stick, move the stick out of the cage, taking care not to bump the bird's head on the doorway. Some cages are designed with such small openings that the bird will have to duck its head in order to ride out on the stick.

Once you have brought the bird out of its cage on your stick, praise it. You can reward it by bringing it to its favorite play area. Then place the bird back in its cage and repeat the lesson. Once your parrot is willing to mount the stick without hesitancy, you can begin to remove the paper from inside the cage. It is important that the paper be removed one sheet at a time for each time the bird performs properly. The very last sheet of paper to be removed is the piece which covers the wire immediately above the door. It is very standard for parrots to prevent you from taking them from their cage by grabbing it with their beaks just as they are going through the doorway. Once they hook the wire, they are able to lift themselves off of your stick and climb back into the cage or onto the top of the cage. They usually act very proud of themselves when they foil your attempt to move them somewhere. Placing a piece of paper over this area will prevent your bird from being able to hook onto the wire. By the time you remove this last piece, your pet will have practiced leaving its cage on your stick enough to accept the procedure.

STEP TEN—STEP FROM INSIDE OF CAGE TO HAND

When your parrot is willing to leave its cage on demand whenever the stick is offered, it is time to substitute your hand. Try offering your hand at the next lesson instead of the stick. If the bird does not accept your hand and tries to avoid you, it will be necessary to repeat the papering exercise. When your pet is willing to accept your hand each time, you have succeeded in hand-taming your bird. Congratulations to you both!

LIVING WITH A TAME PARROT

It is a very welcome sight to approach your parrot's cage and

Lesser sulfur-crested cockatoo. Once your pet is hand-tamed, it will look forward to the times it is let out of the cage.

see the bird raise its foot in hopes that you will open the door and pick it up! Parrots that have been tamed to this level usually love to spend as much time outside of their cage as you will allow. You can continue to reinforce the taming you have accomplished by always carrying the bird from the inside of its cage to the top or to its playground whenever you allow the bird time for freedom and exercise. Obviously, the bird is fully capable of getting out of the cage itself and may even choose to return there for food or water during the period it is allowed out. However, by actively carrying the bird just from the inside of the cage to the outside when you open the door, you are using freedom to reinforce the lessons learned.

Now that your bird is hand-tamed, you can develop a comfortable routine with your pet. For example, my birds know that I will let them out of their cage as soon as I get up in the morning and when I return home from work in the evening. Consequently, I always have pets who welcome my return and are quite anxious to see me. I thor-

Blue and yellow macaw. A hand-tame parrot is a pet that can enjoy more and more time with its human family—it can become a true companion.

oughly enjoy the welcome I receive. Another benefit is that I can sleep in on weekend mornings because the birds know that they will get out once they hear me move about the house. If the house is quiet, they stay quiet. Your pet will be most comfortable if you develop routines for it. Routines offer your parrot the security of knowing what to expect. You gain by having a pet who is calm and friendly.

You can also include your pet in more of your activities. Since you know that the bird will respond to your request to mount your hand on demand, you have control over your pet. You can have fun interacting with the bird without being in a training situation. You can just enjoy each other's company and develop a rewarding relationship. Eventually, your pet may become so attached to you that it will want to be near you whenever you are home. Many owners place perches around their home so that their pet can spend time with them in any room in the house. Other parrots spend much of their time riding around on their owner's shoulder or inside a vest or sweater. (If you choose to have your bird on your shoulder, be very cautious that the bird does not bite your face. You could be seriously hurt.) Once you have hand-tamed your parrot, your relationship can develop in any direction which works for the two of you. Parrots can be very fun and lively companions. Do enjoy your friend's company.

44

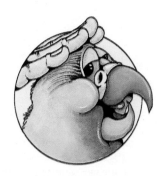

Your parrot may be so comfortable with you once you complete the hand-taming exercises that it will welcome your offer to pet it. Cockatoos are often very anxious to be petted. As a rule, these birds enjoy being petted so much that they have been dubbed "the lap dog of the bird world." However, some parrots will resist being petted. They may be very willing to mount your hand as trained, but they want nothing else to do with your hand. Amazon parrots often behave this way at first.

PETTING

Petting a bird is different than training. When you were giving your bird its lessons, you trained the bird that it *had* to do the specific act you trained it to perform. Petting a bird is a giving and receiving of affection. The bird does not have to be affectionate. You will need to develop a genuine friendship with your pet before it will allow you to touch it.

Individual parrots vary in how much they like to be petted and where they like to be petted. Most Amazons thoroughly enjoy having their heads, ears, and necks stroked with a single finger but may resist having your hand on their back. Cockatoos generally love being petted and stroked on their heads and backs and often beg for more when you stop. A hand-fed baby will often enjoy any affection you are willing to give if you spend time with your bird each day. These loving birds may even enjoy being snuggled.

You can offer to pet your friend when it is perched on a free-standing perch or on your hand. It is generally easiest to pet your bird when it is perched on your arm and your arm is close to your body. The bird will feel quite secure next to you and is more likely to accept your touch. Gently touch your finger to the bird's head or back very lightly. If the bird does not like having you do that, it may snarl, whirl around with its beak open in warning, or flee. A tame bird will usually react mildly. It just wants to tell you that it does not like your action. It is very unlikely that you will be bitten unless you ignore the warnings.

Keep trying each day or so. Eventually, your pet will realize that your touch is not unpleasant or painful and will learn that it actually is very comforting and pleasant. Parrots are very social creatures. They spend a lot of time in their natural flocks preening each other and showing affection. If you do not have a second parrot, your bird will crave for that kind of affection from you.

When you observe your pet fluffing the feathers around its head and rubbing the exposed end of a perch or toy, you have found a time when the bird will be more receptive to having its head rubbed. Gently approach the bird and offer your finger near its head. If your pet lowers its head and fluffs its feathers, your invitation has been accepted. The feathers are fluffed to allow your finger to touch the skin directly. This appears to be more pleasant for the parrot than having you simply stroke its sleek feathers. Usually, the birds thoroughly enjoy having your finger caress them near their ear coverts (the rows of small feathers which hide the ear opening on each side of the head), at the feathers just above their beaks, and underneath their beaks on their throats.

When you have established an excellent relationship, you may discover that your pet wants to "caress" or "preen" you. Your parrot may pick up strands of your hair and run it through its beak as

Below: Amazon parrots, like this blue-fronted Amazon, enjoy having their heads scratched. **Opposite:** A stunning scarlet macaw.

it does with its own feathers. Parrots are very fastidious about their personal hygiene and they welcome the assistance from their mates to preen their head. Parrots are very comforted by having their mates preen them. Often, you can observe a parrot asking its mate for this affection. This mutual preening helps to cement the relationship between the two birds. You have been honored that your bird thinks so highly of you to offer to preen you.

Salmon-crested cockatoo. Cockatoos seem to love petting more than other parrots, and they generally don't mind hands on their backs.

DISCIPLINE

Articles and advertisements about parrots are quick to point out the many positive features of having parrots as pets. They talk about the small amounts of space that these birds need, the minimal care requirements when compared to a dog, and the intelligence and beauty of these exotic birds. As you have no doubt discovered, there are a number of drawbacks to owning parrots as well as these attractive features. They can be very loud. No article will lovingly describe the beautiful call of a parrot. Parrots are loud and obnoxious. Parrots are messy. In their natural world where food is abundant, they simply drop the morsel that no longer interests them and take another. Just because you are paying for that food and have to clean up after them is no reason for the bird to change its comfortable habit. Parrots can also be destructive. Their need to chew can seem insatiable and they may grab anything in reach to satisfy that need. Nothing is sacred to those beaks. Lastly, parrots can be nippy and obnoxious at times towards their owners.

It is very possible to live with a pet with such mixed blessings. You can train the bird not to exhibit some of its obnoxious habits and provide safe outlets for others. Some faults you may just have to accept in order to have the bird share your home. In the end, it is a very personal choice. Parrots are living creatures with their own unique lifestyles. If you and your parrot can accept each other, you have the basis for an excellent relationship. If this type of pet simply does not meet all of your needs, then sell the bird with a clear conscience and select a pet which you will enjoy. The following sections review some of the common problems associated with having a parrot live in your home, discuss why the bird behaves in this manner and offer several solutions.

SCREAMING

Some parrots have a very loud call and often enjoy screaming immensely. Morning and evening are the most common times for screaming. Typically, parrots are very quiet during midday and through the night. Wild-caught African greys and most cockatoos may be the worst offenders for noise. However, none of the parrots will win any awards for a beautiful voice.

Screaming can be controlled if you are able to allow some

49

time when the bird can safely be allowed to scream. Because of this need, owning a parrot is not recommended if you live in close proximity to neighbors who like peace and quiet. My birds scream to their hearts' content after they are let out of their cages in the morning. Nothing seems to stop them until the daily ration of screaming is out of their system. Usually, the screaming session only lasts 15 to 20 minutes and then it is over until a short burst around dinner time. You can provide other safe times to "chatter." Many birds will enjoy "singing" along with the radio or TV or any other noisy activity in your home. If you allow your pet this free time, you can demand quiet at other points in the day. However, if you force your pet to suppress its need to scream at all times, it may develop neurotic behaviors. Again, the more closely you allow your bird to follow its natural daily routine, the more controllable your bird will be.

When your bird chooses to scream at undesirable times, there are several ways to handle the situation. First, there are actions you should not take. Do not reward the bird for its bad behavior. Getting angry and shouting at the bird is a reward. You are putting on a very entertaining display. You are also paying attention to the bird. Do not try to bribe the bird into being quiet by offering food in exchange for peace. It won't work for long. All you are doing is training the bird to scream for treats. Do not give the bird a lot of loving attention when it screams in the belief that it is just lonely. You will prove yourself right and find yourself responding to a screaming bird more and more often. Never strike the bird—it accomplishes nothing except to create anger and fear.

To discipline, you can put the bird back into its cage and cover it for about five to ten minutes. When the bird screams inappropriately, tell it to step up onto your hand and then place it in its cage immediately. The bird will lose its freedom because of its actions. The five- to ten-minute penalty is sufficient because birds live in the "here and now." After about ten minutes, they will forget why they are in their cage and nothing more can be gained from the experience. Covering the cage makes the punishment one step more severe by separating the bird from its world visually.

You must take this negative reinforcement period seriously. Completely ignore the bird for the ten minutes it must stay in its cage. This may be difficult. The bird is going to try every possible method to break your heart so you will open the door. Parrots can look so adorable and cute when they want something from you, but it is just a trick. Harden your heart for the five to ten minutes. You can adore your pet again after the period of confinement. Your pet must learn

A pair of *Forpus* parrots. Keep in mind that chattering and screeching is part of a parrot's daily routine. Your pet should be allowed a supervised screaming session every day.

that *you* determine what is acceptable behavior. Please note that this form of discipline will quickly lose its effectiveness if you forget the bird in its cage for several hours.

If you were giving the bird attention when it began to scream, you can discipline your pet by ignoring it or leaving the room. The negative reinforcement is the loss of your pet's favorite person—you. This is a serious negative reinforcement. The parrot is a social creature and you are its special "preening buddy." Parrots usually do not like to be alone.

Some owners spray a stream of water at their bird's wing to startle the bird. Never aim at the face. Get a bright red or orange water pistol and "shoot" the bird when it needs discipline. Your parrot will quickly associate the unpleasant experience with the bright water pistol and not the water. You may notice that you simply need to get the pistol ready and your pet will stop the undesirable behavior.

Sometimes a loud "No!" is effective. If you associate the "No!" with something that the bird does not like, the word becomes quite effective. For example, if you begin to discipline by sharply saying "No!" and then place the bird in its cage and cover it, the bird will begin to associate the word "No!" with the bad experience of losing its freedom. Soon, you will discover that a sharp "No!" solves the problem.

You can manage the screaming on a long-term basis by putting the screams on cue. For example, you can induce your bird to scream by making similar sounds yourself or talking to your pet very loudly. Birds who are interested in screaming will usually join in quickly. They like to chatter with you and seem to enjoy the "conversation." This activity accomplishes two functions. First, it provides a safe time for the bird to be noisy and second, it gives the bird a consistent time when it knows that you will give it your undivided attention. Once the bird is used to this activity, you control screaming at undesirable times by not giving the cue. Simply don't talk loudly to the bird when you don't want it to scream. This technique works to some degree; it is not always successful. However, it has worked well enough in my household to keep everyone peaceful. I have a noisy "conversation" with my birds as soon as I come home in the evening. It only lasts a few minutes. Then I can have a very tranquil evening. If I fail to greet the birds, they get very upset and carry on until we "talk." At that point, it usually takes longer to settle them.

DESTRUCTIVENESS

Parrots love to chew. Their beaks grow continuously and they need to exercise them many hours per day to keep them whittled down to the right size. This is another habit that you will not be able to train a bird to end. However, you can control it. Provide your pet with enough toys to keep its beak happy. Your bird will appreciate variety. Your pet should have a climbing tree for both chewing and climbing. You can select a small limb or bush from a nearby wooded area, remove the leaves, clean it thoroughly and give it to your pet— if you are sure the area has not been sprayed with chemicals for several years. The leftover pieces of lumber from a nearby lumber yard are usually free and can give your pet hours of fun. Many pet stores sell different kinds of toys. These offer lots of variety but tend to be expensive. You can fold up pieces of brown paper and let your bird rip them to shreds. The list of possibilities is almost endless. Those beaks are very strong and parrots love to play. Be careful that you only provide items which either cannot be ingested or natural fibers which will not be harmful if swallowed by the bird.

In spite of all of your good efforts at providing toys, you will have to keep temptation out of reach. Keep the birds in their cages when you cannot be there to supervise their activities. When you allow them free time, keep your furniture, lamps, rugs, and drapes out of reach. Cover electrical outlets and keep all cords out of the area. If your walls are covered with wallpaper, your pet may be able to start peeling it off. Non-leaded paint which can easily be scrubbed may be the best wall treatment in the bird's area. Moldings around windows and doors are not safe either. My bird's area is located near a large sliding door covered with some drapes I treasure. I prevented damage to the drapes by purchasing a large piece of tempered glass and placing it between the cages and the window. The birds were disciplined every time they tried to sample the glass. They now know the glass is off limits and, consequently, my drapes and window molding have not been touched. The glass has also prevented sprayed food from landing on the drapes.

Salmon-crested cockatoo. All parrots are notorious chewers. Your pet must be provided with safe items to gnaw, as chewing wears down the continuously growing beak.

You will have to be on your guard or accept that some of your furniture will be damaged. In spite of our constant vigilance, a good chair was accidentally pushed too close to my bird's cage by a visitor. In just two minutes, Carly, my cockatoo, inflicted some serious damage to the upholstery.

Cockatoos may be the worst offenders in the chewing department. You may never be able to get to a level of training where you feel that you can trust the bird alone. Never put a cockatoo in a wooden cage or in an outdoor aviary with a dirt floor. It is almost guaranteed that the bird will escape. You must even be sure that the metal caging you select is sturdy enough. Cockatoos can patiently chew on a single area for hours at a time. We like to joke that cockatoos should have been named "flying chainsaws."

Amazons love to chew but are usually satisfied with the toys you provide. They are much less inclined to damage your furnishings. Once you know your bird, you may be able to trust it enough to leave it in its play area without constant supervision. You are still taking a risk, but the odds are better that nothing will be damaged. The other types of parrots are in-between the extremes of the Amazon and the cockatoo. Again, there will be individual differences.

Peach-fronted conure and a cockatiel. Biting occurs for several reasons. Before punishing your pet, try to figure out what caused the bite in the first place.

Blue and yellow macaw. When you are bitten by your parrot, pull your finger up and away and tell the bird "No!" in a sharp tone of voice.

BITING

There are many reasons why parrots bite. The one you have most certainly encountered so far is the bite of a frightened, untamed bird. In this case, biting is simply a means of protection. The parrot is afraid of you or the action you are doing and wants to get away. You should not punish an untamed bird who bites simply because it is frightened. The bird will not understand your punishment. However, you do not have to tolerate being bitten. Say "No!" sharply and pull away.

Once your pet is tamed and comfortable in your home, there are many other reasons why it may bite. Fear can still play a role in a tamed parrot. Parrots do not always accept a new person or situation readily. Your pet may actually bite you out of fear or frustration. A change in the location of your pet's cage, a new perch, the addition of a new pet or member of the household are all threats to your pet's established environment. Allow your friend to have a few quiet days to observe the household and accept the changes. You will notice that your bird's behavior will change while it is trying to understand the new situation. The playing and activity will lessen. The bird may appear to be frightened. Often the feathers look very sleek rather than fluffy because they are being held tight against the body. You may notice that the shoulders tend to be more visible. When your pet is acting this way, it is advisable to keep yourself and your friends out of any situation which may cause one of you to be bitten. Your pet is not sure of his world and is feeling defensive. If you should be bitten during this period, do not punish your pet. Your parrot is really just telling you how upset it is. After a few days, everything will settle into a normal routine and your happy, responsive friend will emerge once again.

Another common problem is jealousy. Often a parrot will decide that one person in the household is its special person or "preening buddy." Then everyone else in the household becomes an enemy because they take the special person away from the parrot. The parrot can respond to the other members of the household in a very vindictive manner. The bird may choose to attack the "enemy" or even the object of his affection if the special person chooses to spend time with someone else. When biting is used to get to point across to the world that the parrot is jealous of his special person's affections, the bites can be very serious. The bird is intending to hurt. Other aggressive behaviors include lunging, striking or impressive displays of raised feathers, open wings and an open beak.

The only way to control this type of behavior is to refuse to tolerate it. Once the parrot is tamed, see that the bird spends time with each member of the household and is exposed to visitors. When any unacceptable behavior is displayed, say "No!" and return the bird to its cage for ten minutes of confinement. Do not coddle the bird when it acts aggressively towards another person. Petting the bird and encouraging it with your voice will only reinforce the bad behavior.

Dominance behavior can cause some birds to bite aggressively. Remember that parrots are still wild animals. Nature has programmed them to organize their world into a pecking order. Every bird wants to be in the highest position and will do anything to achieve that goal. To maintain control over your pet, you must be in the dominant position. Additionally, you must ensure that your pet understands that everyone else in your household is in a more dominant position than the parrot. If you have one person in your family who refuses to make the bird behave, your parrot will probably pick on that person mercilessly.

Macaws have a particularly annoying way of establishing dominance. They try to jab people with the point of their beaks. While this is not biting, it is just as unpleasant. You can control this behavior by taking the bird to the veterinarian or to a trained bird handler and having the tip of the bird's beak dulled. Macaws are fiercely proud of their sharp beaks; an individual can spend hours rubbing its beak on the sides of branches to keep it sharp. After you have the beak dulled, the bird will know that the beak is no longer a sharp point and will not try to jab you with it. This procedure is very similar to wing-clipping. It

Blue and yellow macaw. Parrots often use their beaks to balance on a perch or a hand or arm. This action should not be confused with biting.

does not damage the bird and after a few months the bird's beak will again become sharp. It also takes away one of the bird's advantages which helps you to stay in the dominant position.

Sexual maturity can turn your friendly, gentle pet into an aggressive fiend. Luckily, most parrots only act aggressive during the breeding season. This is generally in the early spring time, but aggressive behavior can be seen at other times of the year. If you have more than one bird and birds of opposite sexes, your mature parrot will display and approach the other bird. If you have a single bird, it may try to approach you. Parrot sexual displays include fluffing the feathers and fanning tails, snapping the wings, regurgitating food, dilating the pupils and making a clucking noise not heard other times of the year. If someone who is not the object of its affection approaches the bird, a serious bite could be inflicted.

The breeding season can last a few weeks to several months. Do not hide the bird in a corner and stop all activities during this period. Your bird will probably need more activity than usual so that it does not get bored and give in to the aggressive feelings. Keep your friend busy. Handle your pet often, but for very short periods. Be very aware of its attention span. When my Amazon acts obnoxious during breeding season, we joke that his blood must be as thick as pea soup with all of those hormones floating around. Be very careful when you handle your bird at this time. The worst bite I have ever received happened when I offered my Amazon a piece of his favorite food at the wrong time and he grabbed my finger instead. Keep your bird off of your shoulders to insure that the bird is not in the dominant position and cannot reach your face. You cannot trust a mature bird during breeding season. When the season is over, it is very likely that your old friend will be back.

Some parrots become permanently aggressive once they mature. If you are unfortunate enough to own such a bird, you may want to sell it to a breeder or place the bird in an aviary.

A tame bird who shares a cage with another parrot may start to bite for no obvious reason. This bird is becoming more dependent on the company of the other bird and resents your intrusion. Spend more time handling each bird individually to maintain your position as a friend. If you have the space, you may want to place each bird in its own cage for a while.

Biting is a complex behavior. You need to understand your pet's situation in order to determine whether the bite was caused by aggression, fear, or hormones. Aggression should never be tolerated. Biting in fear should not be punished. Spend time observing your pet and learning about it. As you get to know your pet, you will be able to determine what caused the biting episode and then handle it appropriately.

Salmon-crested cockatoo. The more you become acquainted with your pet and his behavior, the more comfortable the both of you will be.

Many owners value the ability of their parrots to mimic human words and phrases. You can certainly have a lot of fun with birds who "talk." In one busy household, the resident African grey noticed that whenever the telephone rang, someone would yell "I'll get it!" and rush to answer. Soon he learned to yell "I'll get it!" in the voice of each family member. Several times confusion reigned as everyone thought someone else was going to answer the phone!

SPEECH TRAINING

Some parrots can acquire a large vocabulary. Mimicking 200 words and phrases is not uncommon. In some species, however, the parrots will never utter a single word in spite of the owner's patient lessons. There is no guarantee that speech training will succeed. Each individual parrot must feel inclined to "talk." Some species of parrots are better talkers than others. African greys are clearly the best as a generality. Macaws and Amazons are reasonable talkers. Cockatoos are generally the least interested in mimicry. However, I have met cockatoos who talked constantly and greys who would not say a word. If you feel that mimicry is an important attribute for your pet, select a bird who has already demonstrated an inclination to "talk." There is still no guarantee that this bird will choose to talk in your home, but the odds of success are far greater.

The first word is the hardest word to teach. Generally, after the first word is mimicked successfully, other words follow quickly. You may have to be careful of what you say in the presence of your pet. You will never know which words your bird may choose to mimic. You also never know exactly when those words will be said at a later time. Suffice it to say that some owners have been placed in embarrassing situations because of their talkative parrots!

The first rule of teaching mimicry is repetition. You will have to repeat the word you want your pet to say many, many times. The joke in my household is that I know how to say "hello" very well now as I have practiced it so much. Unfortunately, my Amazon does not seem too inclined to try it himself.

It helps if you say the word in the same manner that a parrot would say it. It is unlikely that your pet will learn his first word if you simply say it in your normal tone of voice. A flat "Hello" will not pique your pet's interest. However, if you put lots of excitement into your voice and really drag out the word as you say it, your pet will probably take notice. Find a parrot in your area who talks and really listens to the bird. Try imitating the bird's voice. Your pet will be most responsive to this type of voice. If your pet is interested, it may approach you and watch your mouth intently as you make this interesting sound.

When your parrot makes a sound that is very close to what you wanted, reward the effort with a morsel of your pet's favorite food as soon as the bird makes the sound. This positive reinforcement will encourage your pet to make the sound again in hopes of getting another treat. You can also pet your bird if being touched is something the bird truly enjoys. Be sure you select a reinforcement which the bird really wants.

It is possible to teach a bird to talk by playing a continuous tape recording of the word or phrase you want the bird to learn. While this method is certainly convenient and much less tedious than saying the word yourself hundreds of times, it has two serious drawbacks. First, you have not taught the bird to say the word in your presence. The bird may say the word all day long and then become mute as soon as you enter the house. Secondly, you are not there to reinforce the bird's efforts. You are depending on the bird's own amusement to make it continue to say the word in the practice sessions. However, if you are there to reinforce the efforts of mimicry as they happen, you are greatly increasing the chances that your pet will take a keener interest in speech. Efforts are much more fun when a treat appears in response.

Peach-fronted conure. Food rewards make speech training a lot easier and more successful. Be sure to offer your pet his particular favorites.

Salmon-crested cockatoo. Keep in mind that your pet's initial attempt to repeat your word will not be perfect. Reward the bird when he gets close to the proper sound.

After the bird repeats the phrase whenever you say it, you should only provide a treat as a reinforcement on a random basis. Once the word is learned, the bird will not try very hard if it knows that it will always get a treat for every effort, no matter how small. Move to a random reinforcement now. Sometimes you will reinforce the word and sometimes you will require the bird to say it several times before you reinforce the effort by providing the treat. Random reinforcement is used after the word is fully learned to ensure that the bird continues to try. Parrots are lazy by nature. If they know that you will reward them for any effort, no matter how small, their efforts will diminish. However, if you move to randomized reinforcement, you maintain interest and effort.

When you decide to teach the bird a second phrase, be sure that you only reinforce the bird for saying the word you want at that particular time. For example, the bird knows "Hello" and will repeat it on command. You decide to teach the phrase "How are you?" next. When you say "How are you?" your pet can only respond with something close to that phrase to receive a treat. If the bird says "Hello," do not reinforce that sound. It is not what you wanted to hear. Reinforce only the efforts you want. You can only teach one thing at a

The African grey parrot is generally considered to be the most talented talker of the entire parrot family. All parrots are individuals, however, and not all African greys are great orators.

time. If your pet knows exactly what you want, it will learn much faster. If you decide that any sound is good enough, you will have a very difficult time teaching your parrot more words. Your pet knows that it does not have to learn.

Once your pet has mastered some words, reinforce the parrot when it says them in front of other people. Most owners want their birds to talk in order to show friends their interesting pet. Unfortunately, most parrots will become completely mute in the presence of strangers. If you reinforce any efforts to vocalize in front of other people, your bird will soon understand that talking is a desired activity and it may start to talk in front of anyone who comes to your home.

If you have more than one pet, you may notice that your birds are "talking" to each other. All of them will know your standard commands such as "Step up" to mount and "OK" to be released. They may learn to mimic these commands and "train" each other to perform those behaviors. Your birds may teach each other how to talk. My trainer's birds only learned their first word from her. They learned the others from her oldest parrot who had a large vocabulary.

Have fun with your talking birds. Most guests will not expect your pet to talk so you can have tremendous fun surprising and amusing them. The stories will make great conversation for years.

With consistent care and love, your relationship with your parrot should continue to improve long after the formal training has been completed. The taming and training exercises allowed each of you to learn what responses to anticipate from the other in most situations. You both learned that those responses would not cause any fear or pain. In short, you learned to trust each other. Because training provided the basis for trust to develop, it was possible for a friendship to begin.

CONCLUSION

It is now up to you to continue to develop that relationship in a way which meets your needs. Your relationship is only dependent on your level of interest and your pet's health. Enjoy your pet. Include it in as many of your activities as are safely possible and will be fun for both of you. As your pet learns to respond to the stimulation and fun, it will become a more lively and interesting friend. You may discover that each year you enjoy your friend even more. I hope this is true for you. These beautiful birds are to be enjoyed. Your life should be richer for the experience.

Blue and yellow macaw. Once you and your parrot learn to trust each other, anything is possible. The two of you will be good friends for many years.

INDEX

A blue and yellow macaw about to go for a ride on his master's hand.